Investigating Medieval Times

By Alison Honey and Anita Ganeri

Illustrated by Peter Stevenson

CONTENTS

Introduction

The word 'medieval' comes from the Latin for Middle Ages. This book, which focuses on life in England, starts with the invasion of William, Duke of Normandy and the Battle of Hastings in 1066, and ends with another battle, when Henry Tudor defeated Richard III at Bosworth Field in 1485. Scotland throughout the period was a separate kingdom, uniting with England much later on, in 1603. Military expeditions were made into Wales and Ireland but neither was fully conquered.

European historians think of the Middle Ages as the filling in the sandwich between classical times and the age of the rebirth of classical ideas, the Renaissance.

But historians don't all agree when the period began and ended. Some say medieval times began when the Roman Empire broke up in the fourth and fifth centuries, others put the date five hundred years later.

The English face the Norman invasion

How we investigate

Our knowledge of this time comes from lots of different sources:
- Written accounts such as manuscripts, bills and documents, eyewitness reports of battles, chronicles
- paintings, embroideries (see the Bayeux Tapestry, *left*) and stained-glass windows
- tombs and effigies
- medieval buildings and remains
- archaeology – clues on the land.

The Battle of Hastings

William, Duke of Normandy, and Harold, King of the English, led their forces into battle on 14 October 1066, near the present day town of Hastings in Sussex. In a long, hard battle, Harold and many of his army died. Two months later, William, whom we call 'the Conqueror' was crowned King and England became part of his Anglo-Norman empire.

England after 1066

This was a period of constant warring. When William the Conqueror's son, Henry I, died in 1135 his only surviving child was a daughter, Matilda. The idea that a woman might rule as Queen in her own right was challenged by her cousin, Stephen. England was plunged into civil war until Matilda's son, Henry, Count of Anjou, was recognised as her heir. In 1154, on the death of Stephen, he became Henry II.

The Angevins

Besides being Count of Anjou, Henry II married the heiress, Eleanor of Aquitaine and acquired vast areas of land in southern France.

Their son Richard was known as the Lionheart because of his valour on the battlefield. His younger brother John has gone down in history as one of the wicked kings of England. He was not a very successful king – he lost Normandy to the King of France, and was forced to sign the Magna Carta in 1215 giving over power to his barons.

Richard I became King of England in 1189, but spent most of his reign fighting the Crusades in the Holy Land. The lions in his coat-of-arms were a symbol of his bravery.

The Hundred Years' War

Edward I, who reigned from 1272 to 1307, turned his warlike ambitions to Wales and Scotland, but his grandson Edward III returned to the battlefields of France, seeking to win back his ancestors' lands. One of his greatest victories was the battle of Crécy, 1346, where his son Edward, known as the Black Prince, established his military reputation.

It was a great start to the long campaign of the Hundred Years' War, and a further boost was provided in 1415 when Henry V won a famous victory at Agincourt, enabling his son to be crowned King of France. But in the end all the victories won by the English came to nothing.

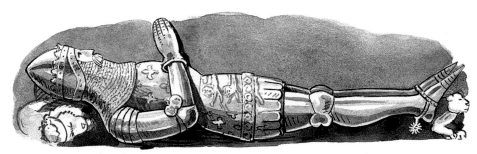

The tomb of the Black Prince in Canterbury Cathedral

Lancaster and York

While Henry I had no son to succeed him, Edward III had the opposite problem – too many sons. His eldest, the Black Prince, died before him, so that Edward was succeeded by his grandson, Richard II. When he proved a weak ruler, Edward III's other sons began to quarrel about who should reign in his place.

Richard II was deposed by his cousin Henry of Lancaster, who became the first Lancastrian king, Henry IV in 1399. But others, notably descendants of the Duke of York, also felt they had a claim to the throne.

Wars of the Roses

Henry IV's grandson was only a small boy when he succeeded to the throne and was soon deposed by his cousin, Edward of York. This was a civil war that became known as the Wars of the Roses: the Lancastrians wore red roses, the Yorkists, white. Disputes between Lancaster and York ended in 1485 when Richard III, of York, lost his throne to Henry Tudor, representing the Lancastrian faction, at the Battle of Bosworth Field, in Leicestershire.

Medieval Society

William I's conquest of England allowed him to reward his followers with land. He declared that he owned all the land in England and, in return for giving parts of this to about 180 barons or 'tenants-in-chief', he expected their loyalty and support in wartime. These barons in turn divided their land among knights who promised to fight for them when required. The knights lent land to the peasants who either worked for the lord of the manor or paid rent. This method of dividing up land was known as the feudal system.

Life as a peasant

The peasants were either 'free' – and paid rent to the lord – or they were 'unfree'. The unfree peasants were called serfs and had to work several days of the week for the lord for no pay. However, if a serf ran away and avoided recapture by his lord for a year and a day he was granted his freedom.

This was what was expected of the people who tenanted the land surrounding Corfe Castle in Dorset:

'When there may happen to be war in the neighbourhood of the castle, the tenents of the town ought to be in the castle for forty days at their own charges for the defence of the same castle, and this as service for the tenure of their lands.'

Fourteenth-century account, quoted in Corfe Castle Guidebook, The National Trust, 1995, p.50

Law and order

The lord of the manor and his officers were responsible for law and order on his land. Less serious crimes were tried at the manor court. Serious offenders went to the shire courts to be tried by the sheriff, who was appointed by the king. There was a separate court for judging members of the Church.

A *manor* was the land belonging to a nobleman. *Shires* were like the counties we have today. Each shire had a sheriff.

A woman's lot

With very rare exceptions, women in the Middle Ages had few rights. A woman was considered to be first the property of her father, then of her husband. Peasant women worked hard, raising their children, spinning, weaving and helping in the fields – few lived to old age.

Noblewomen had servants to run the house and did not work but were often in charge of their husbands' estates while they were away at war. Something which both rich and poor women held in common was the danger of childbirth, during which death was not unusual.

For better or for worse

Among noble families, marriage was looked on as a business contract and usually involved a *dowry* (money or objects given by the family of the bride to the bridegroom). An only daughter was viewed as a great catch because when her father died she – and her husband – inherited the family's wealth.

Margaret Paston, quoted in *Medieval Britain* by Walter Robson, OUP, 1991, p.90

Here is part of a letter from a member of a wealthy Norfolk family, writing to her husband in late medieval times (1462):

'When I was in Norwich this week, I called at my mother's. While I was there Mr Wrothe came in. He saw our daughter, who was with me, and said she was a fine-looking girl... He said that he knew a young man from a good family who has an income of £200 a year. He is 18 years old. What do you think about the idea? My mother thinks that if we wait any longer we will have to pay a bigger dowry.'

Royal weddings

Royal marriages were nearly always made for political reasons. This is what one chronicler wrote about Henry I's scheme when his daughter Matilda married the Count of Anjou in France in 1128:

'It is true and not to be denied that King Henry gave his daughter in marriage with a politic design, that he might establish peace more surely and securely between the Normans and the Angevins, who had often troubled each other from disputes.'

Gesta Stephani, quoted in *The Normans in Britain*, by Donald Wilkinson & John Cantrell, Macmillan, 1987, p.82

When her father died Matilda's marriage led to civil war – she had to bring her army across from Anjou to fight Stephen, William the Conqueror's grandson, for her throne.

A more fruitful royal marriage was that of Matilda's son, Henry II, to the French princess Eleanor of Aquitaine; this brought most of south-west France under Angevin rule.

The Church

The medieval Church was extremely powerful. At its head was the Pope in Rome. During the eleventh and twelfth centuries the popes challenged the power of kings. In England the most important bishop was the Archbishop of Canterbury. He served two masters, the King and the Pope. The story of Henry II and Thomas Becket, Archbishop of Canterbury, illustrates the conflict between king and pope.

Murder in the cathedral

Henry II wanted the clergy to be tried in the king's courts, not the religious courts. He argued fiercely with Thomas Becket, Archbishop of Canterbury, who had been one of his closest friends and advisers. Thomas asked the Pope for help. This made the quarrel worse. In 1170, in a moment of frustration, Henry is said to have exclaimed 'Who will rid me of this turbulent priest?'. Four of his knights, thinking they were doing their king a favour, rode to Canterbury and murdered the Archbishop in his cathedral.

Henry, who had not intended Becket to be killed, took responsibility for the murder, doing penance in front of the ordinary men and women of Canterbury to show his sadness. In an extraordinary act for a king, he walked barefoot to the cathedral and made the monks whip his bare back. Thomas was made a saint by the Pope in 1173 and his shrine became one of the most famous pilgrimage sites in England.

Hell fire and brimstone

In general people were very religious and attended church even though few could understand the Latin service. Churches displayed pictures to warn of the perils of sinning: wall paintings often showed the Last Judgement – the good welcomed into heaven and sinners tossed into the torment of hell.

UPTON HOUSE (BEARSTED COLLECTION) NTPL / ANGELO HORNAK

This medieval painting shows St Michael slaying the dragon, while the fires of hell burn below.

The Canterbury Tales

Geoffrey Chaucer's *Canterbury Tales*, written about a group of pilgrims on their way to visit the shrine of Thomas Becket, shows how people might have viewed the Church and its representatives in the later Middle Ages.

Chaucer pokes fun at the luxury and corruption of the Church. Do you think we can trust his view?

> *You can compare Chaucer's descriptions of these characters from the Church.*

Workshop to Warfare, CUP, 1983, p.42

The *Sabbath* (Sunday) was meant to be a day of rest leaving people free to go to church and worship. People were punished if they worked on this or on feast days. This is from a 1451 court record:

'Isabella Hunter and Catherine Pykring admit that they washed their linen on St Mary Magdalene Day. They are to have two whippings with a handful of flax.'

The Monk

*'This Monk was therefore a good man to horse;
Greyhounds he had, as swift as birds, to course.
Hunting a hare or riding at a fence
Was all his fun, he spared for no expense.'*

The Pardoner

*'He had a cross of metal set with stones
And, in a glass, a rubble of pigs' bones.
And with these relics, any time he found
Some poor up-country parson to astound,
On one short day, in money down, he drew
More than the parson in a month or two.'*

(The Pardoner was authorised by the Pope to sell pardons to people who wanted their sins forgiven)

The Parson

*'Holy and virtuous he was, but then
Never contemptuous of sinful men,
Never disdainful, never too proud or fine,
But was discreet in teaching and benign.
His business was to show a fair behaviour
and draw men thus to Heaven and their Saviour.'*

Geoffrey Chaucer, *The Canterbury Tales*, trans. Neville Coghill, Penguin, 1968, pp.24, 33, 38

Monastic Life

For most people, the centre of their religious life was the local parish church, but, where they existed, *monasteries* (houses for monks or nuns) played a big part in local life.

The Cistercians

This order of monks, founded in France, tended to establish monasteries in isolated areas where they had little contact with people outside. William of Malmesbury, an English monk, wrote about them in 1135:

'The abbot allows himself no extra luxuries, wherever he is he is equally sparing of food and of speech; for never more than two dishes are served either to him or to his company; lard and meat never but to the sick. From September to Easter they only eat one meal a day except on Sunday... While they take care of the stranger and sick, they inflict terrible punishments on their own bodies for the health of their souls.'

Fountains Abbey Teacher's Book, The National Trust, 1991

NTPL / GEORGE WRIGHT

Buckland Abbey in Devon was established as a Cistercian monastery in 1278 by a wealthy widow, Amicia, Countess of Devon, offering the monks an isolated location.

Fountains Abbey

The largest Cistercian monastery in Britain, Fountains Abbey in Yorkshire, was established by 13 monks in 1132. The Archbishop of York gave the monks some land in Skelldale, described as 'more fit for wild beasts than men to inhabit'.

The monks wore habits of undyed sheep's wool and had to observe long periods of silence, communicating only in sign language. The monastery was headed by an Abbot and below him came the choir monks and the laybrothers.

The laybrothers were men who had taken religious vows but worked as farmhands, shepherds, masons or labourers on the Abbey's estates, leaving the choir monks free for their prayers and devotion. The laybrothers were allowed more food and longer hours of sleep and didn't have to go to as many services.

Matins	Midnight
Lauds	2.30am
Prime	5.00am
Terce	9.00am
Sext	Midday
Nones	3.00pm
Vespers	6.00pm
Compline	9.00pm

Daily services for monks at Fountains Abbey

A nun's life

Convents tended to be sited in towns, with the nuns being more involved in local life than the isolated monks. Being a nun provided a living for some wealthier women who had not got married. Becoming a nun, or a monk, was not cheap – the family had to pay money to be accepted and supply a *habit* (clothes), a bed and furniture.

Wealth in wool

Fountains Abbey was involved in mining lead and working iron, quarrying stone, cattle and horse breeding, but its great wealth came from the thousands of sheep which grazed the estates it acquired as it became richer.

In 1200 there were about 100 monks, 500 laybrothers and 15,000 sheep and by the middle of the thirteenth century it was one of the richest religious houses in Britain. Only 100 years after it had been founded by monks craving a more simple life, the Abbey's character had changed completely.

Each novice had her head shaved to show she had given up worldly things, but convent life was not always particularly religious, as shown by this letter written by the Bishop of Winchester in 1387:

'*...some of the nuns of your house bring with them to church, birds, rabbits, hounds, and such like frivolous things... and give more heed [take more notice of them] than to the offices of the church.*'

Workshop to Warfare, CUP, 1983, p.16

Changing times

The fourteenth century was a difficult time for Fountains Abbey, with bad harvests, epidemics of sheep and cattle diseases and the Black Death (see page 22). This killed off many laybrothers, so crucial to running the estate, and as a result many of the Abbey's lands were leased out. The Abbey survived, only to be closed down in 1539 because of Henry VIII's break with the Pope.

Helping the needy

All monasteries and convents gave food to the poor, particularly on feast days. At the Abbey of Lacock in Wiltshire the nuns noted that:

'*We ought to feed on All Soul's day as many as there are ladies, to each poor person a dry loaf and as a relish two herrings or a slice of cheese.*'

Workshop to Warfare, CUP, 1983, p.19

The Medieval Estate

In 1086 William the Conqueror ordered a complete survey of his lands so that he could find out what people owned, in order to raise accurate land taxes and rents. This survey was known as the Domesday Book and is our most important source of information about life in eleventh-century England.

Domesday Book

'They inquired what the manor was called, who held it... who holds it now; how many hides there are; how many ploughs in demesne [a manor house with lands next to it not let out to tenants] and how many belonging to the men; how many villeins; how many cottars; how many slaves; how many freemen; how many sokemen [all types of peasant]; how much woodland; how much meadow; how much pasture...'

Prologue to the Ely Inquest, quoted in *The Normans in Britain* by Donald Wilkinson & John Cantrell, Macmillan, 1987, p.51

A reconstruction of the fifteenth-century Kingston Lacy manor, Dorset

Wimborne Manor

'The king has one manor which is called Wimborne, Shapwick, Crichel, and Up Wimborne... There is land enough for 45 plough teams whilst in demesne the king has 5 plough teams and the farmers have 22 between them. On the whole manor the king has 63 larger farms, 68 small farmers, 125 serfs and 7 cottagers. There are 3 pack horses, 30 pigs, 250 sheep and 44 goats. Eight mills on the manor render £5.10s between them and there are 7 miles of woodland about 1½ miles wide, 150 acres of meadow and 9 miles of pasture by 4½ miles.'

Domesday Book, quoted in Kingston Lacy Estate: a resource book for teachers, The National Trust, 1991, p.15

The Domesday entry for the royal manor of Wimborne, now the Kingston Lacy Estate

Medieval moots

We can find out about the workings of a medieval estate from surviving legal documents. Documentary and archaeological evidence shows that the tenants from Wimborne Manor were required to attend meetings six times a year at Cowgrove where matters concerning the running of the estate and justice were considered. These meetings were known as moots.

After hearing cases where peasants had broken the laws of the manor, the court would decide on an appropriate punishment and, unless the crime was severe, the matter would go no further.

Here are Cowgrove moot cases from June 1403 and 1446:

'*Master Roger Coryngham, Dean of Wimborne, is presented to the homage [a number of tenants who rent land from a superior] for making weirs at Denysmill which has restricted the flow of water at Bakkewater. This has now made the lord's mill unable to grind corn and that the lord and his tenants are flooded with water causing great damage. Therefore in mercy he pays 12d.*'

'*John Oak, the forester of Holt, comes to the court and presents that John Buysshop and John Standard had entered into Holt Chase without licence of the king and had carried off various branches from the trees.*'

Life as a tenant

These moot cases show how tenants' lives were controlled by their lord of the manor or their king.

Tenants took their corn to be ground at the manorial mill (usually driven by waterpower) and handed over part of the corn as payment. The manor provided a central bread oven which tenants had to pay to use. Wood was a valuable resource for cooking and heating, so stealing from the forest (as seen in the second case above) was not to be tolerated. However, stealing wood was less serious than poaching deer. Holt Chase was land put aside for hunting by the king and his representatives; anyone else caught hunting deer was blinded or maimed as punishment.

What's in a name?

The court records demonstrate that in the Middle Ages a surname was often used to describe what job a person did and was not necessarily passed down the generations.

Henry Warreyn was the keeper of the warren, and John Oak was the forester – both had names to fit the work they did on the estate.

Castles and Warfare

The Anglo-Saxons had built fortified castles as protection against invaders such as the Vikings. When the Normans arrived in England they soon built new castles to control the lands they had conquered. At first these were very simple with a wooden tower on a mound of earth (motte) overlooking an enclosure (bailey) – both areas were surrounded by a deep ditch and a high wooden fence.

Chirk Castle in North Wales

NTPL / MATTHEW ANTROBUS

Strong stone

In time the Normans rebuilt their castles in stone. Square look-out towers were replaced by circular ones which were stronger and gave the defenders a better all-round view. In the mid-thirteenth century a lower wall, the curtain wall, was sometimes built outside, to create another barrier and to provide a new line of fire.

Attacking forces had a number of devices like the trebuchet, petrary and mangon – basically giant catapults to lob missiles into the castle. Large rocks were ammunition but dung, dead animals or even enemy heads were options. They also dug under walls to make them fall.

Defending the castle

Castles were built with many features to aid defence:
● a moat with drawbridge
● a *portcullis* (iron-grilled gate at the main entrance)
● *meurtrieres* ('murder holes') through which scalding water or hot sand could be poured
● crenellated battlements for archers to fire from the gaps and then take cover
● arrow loops in the walls for archers to fire through.

Corfe Castle

Corfe Castle was an important defensive site long before the Normans – in 978 King Edward was killed there. During the reign of John (1199-1216), England was under threat from France and Corfe, near the south coast, would have been one of the first for Philip II of France to attack if he invaded. Accounts from 1207 and 1214 show defences were increased – the ditch was enlarged and the wall was strengthened with towers.

NTPL / JOE CORNISH

A fortified manor house

The monarch had to grant a licence before a lord could fortify his dwelling. This was so the king could ensure that his barons and knights were not becoming too powerful. Sir Edward Dalyngrigge was granted the following licence in 1385 by Richard II for Bodiam Castle in Sussex:

'...that he may strengthen with a wall of stone and lime, and crenellate and may construct and make into a castle his manor house of Bodiam, near the sea in the county of Sussex, for the defence of the adjacent county and the resistance to our enemies, and may hold his aforesaid house so strengthened and crenellated and made into a castle for himself and his heirs for ever.'

Historic Houses by Adrian Tinniswood, The National Trust, 1991, p.37

Holding court

In medieval England there was no permanent base where the king held court. Instead he and his retinue travelled to various castles, which required a great deal of planning.

A list of stores and furniture to be delivered for a feast in 1346 for Edward III

60 carcasses of salted muttons, of which 30 were putrid

11 tuns of white wine

1 tun of old and weak wine of the fifth year

8 quarters of coarse salt

1 rick of hay, estimated at 12 cart loads

2 empty tuns

2 open tubs

1 hanging bell for the chapel

2 moveable tables

1 dormant table broken and rotten

4 pairs of trestles

Corfe Castle Guidebook, The National Trust, 1995, p.51

Chivalry and heraldry

During the Middle Ages the concept of chivalry was widespread among knights. This was a special code of behaviour with six rules about loyalty, generosity, courtesy, gallantry, honour and moderation. Knights had the right to bear a coat-of-arms (a design used to recognise individuals in battle). This could also be used to decorate a knight's manor house or castle.

13

Life on the Land

The majority of people in medieval Europe lived in the countryside, surviving off the land. In England there were only about ten towns with a population of over 2,000, and most people lived outside them.

Peasant farmers

In the parts of Britain which had good soil for crops – chiefly the south and central areas – peasants used the 'open field system' of farming. Each village would have three fields divided into long thin strips about eight metres wide and up to a furlong (0.2km) in length.

The strips were divided between the peasant families of the village who were responsible for the crops, although everyone would work together at ploughing, sowing and harvesting times. While two fields were planted with crops like wheat or beans, the third would be grazed with livestock to fertilise the soil – this was called 'lying fallow'. The following year a different field would be left fallow so that the soil did not become exhausted.

NTPL / JOE CORNISH

The medieval field system is still in use near Rhossili, South Wales

The *Vision of Piers the Plowman*, written by William Langland between 1362 and 1399, gives us a few clues as to how tough life was for the average English peasant. This extract deals with the hardships of peasant women:

'Charged with children and overcharged by landlords
What they may spare in spinning, they spend on rental
On milk or on meal to make porridge
To still the sobbing of the children at mealtimes.'

Evidence: The Middle Ages by Jon Nichol & David Downton, Basil Blackwell, 1981, p.23

A hard life

Peasants lived in simple structures made of timber, mud, reeds or slate. The family often shared the house with some livestock. Cooking was done on an open fire with no chimney.

Men and women worked long hours on the land and usually their diet was inadequate for such hard physical labour.

Heavy taxes

In addition to what they owed their lord, peasants had to give a share of their crops (a tenth) to the Church.

This was called a *tithe* and huge Church barns such as Coggeshall in Essex, Buckland Abbey in Devon and Great Coxwell in Oxfordshire were built to house these taxes.

The Peasants' Revolt

For a while after the Black Death, a shortage of labour enabled peasants to ask for higher wages from their lords – some pay doubled.

Evidence: The Middle Ages, p.23

This is what John Gower, a merchant from Kent, wrote about the situation:

'The World goes from bad to worse when shepherd and cowman demand more for their labour than the overseer. Labour is so high priced that those men who employ workers must pay five or six shillings for what used to cost two. Labourers of old did not eat bread made from wheat, their meals were of beans or coarse corn and their drink was water.'

The lords were not happy with this trend and in 1351 a law was passed stating that the levels of pay should be returned to what they were before the Black Death. At the same time the crown increased taxes to help pay for the Hundred Years' War against France. This caused discontent among peasants in Kent and Essex who wanted higher wages and greater freedom.

In 1381 these groups marched on London and were met by Richard II, then only 14 years old; he appeared to agree to many of their requests and the peasants dispersed. However, their leader Wat Tyler was killed and the young king kept none of his promises. The rebellion was put down by the King's supporters, including Sir Edward Dalyngrigge of Bodiam Castle in Sussex.

Language and Literature

Imagine that you were transported back to medieval times – what language would you use to be understood? It would depend on where you lived and what your position was in society.

Which language?

- **LATIN** in monasteries, convents and for church services
- **LATIN** for legal and government documents
- **FRENCH** in castles and manor houses
- **MIDDLE ENGLISH** in countryside and towns

In Scotland and Ireland, dialects based on **GAELIC** (the language of the Celts) were spoken.

NTPL / NICK CARTER

Lacock Abbey
Magna Carta, 1225,
with an official seal

Middle English was a real mix, influenced by the Vikings, Angles, Saxons and Celts. It was common for people not to understand those from a different region.

Gradually Middle English took over from French (except in the Church and at universities where Latin was used). By the end of the fourteenth century English was becoming the language of the ruling classes.

What's in a name?

The English word 'cow' comes from Middle English but beef is from the French 'boeuf'. This might show that the peasants who raised the animals used the English word, but the people who ate the meat were usually the nobles who spoke French.

Spellcheck

The Form of Cury, quoted in *The Art of Dining* by Sara Paston-Williams, The National Trust, 1993, p.58

The spelling of Middle English looks very odd to us now. Here is a medieval recipe from around 1380 for pigeon casserole:

'Take peiouns [pigeons] and stop hem with garlec ypylld [peeled] and with gode erbis ihewe [chopped herbs], and do hem in an erthen pot; cast therto gode broth and whyte grece [lard], powdour fort [a mixture of hot spices such as pepper and ginger], saffron, verious [verjuice] & salt.'

Can you make sense of this Middle English?

Illuminated manuscripts

In major cities and towns in the later Middle Ages scribes would copy works and sell them in stationers' shops. The business of copying books had been restricted to monks who created beautiful, heavily decorated manuscripts, but the work of the scribes meant that books could be seen by more people.

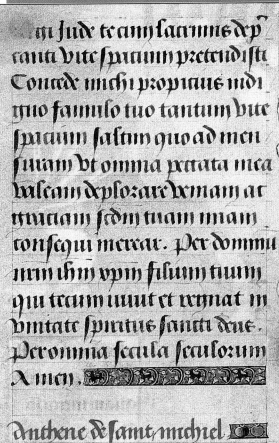

UPTON HOUSE (BEARSTED COLLECTION) NTPL / ANGELO HORNAK

A medieval illuminated manuscript at Upton House in Warwickshire

Printing

In 1477 William Caxton, having learnt the trade of printing in Bruges, opened the first printing press in England.

Caxton printed over 100 different titles including Chaucer's *Canterbury Tales*. Although this was a great step forward, it is important to remember that very few people in England could read.

Arts and Crafts

Much medieval art was connected in some way to the Church: wall paintings, stained glass and decorative stone carving.

Surviving impressions

Examples of medieval art, such as the stained glass panel (*right*) made around 1450 for a Norfolk church, are limited because of the destruction of church contents during the Reformation. This was when the English Church broke away from the Pope's control and monasteries were closed.

Later, during the Commonwealth, sculptures, tombs and windows were attacked with hammers and wall paintings were whitewashed. Thankfully, many medieval manuscripts in libraries were saved.

NTPL / JOHN HAMMOND

Crafts

Here are some unusual examples of the specialist skills of medieval craftspeople:
- **quernpecker** – made the dents on the surface of a millstone
- **wimpler** – made wimples and veils
- **spurrier** – made spurs
- **paternosterer** – made rosary beads

18

Guilds

Craftworkers were encouraged to become members of guilds, to control the quality and price of their goods. There was a structure of membership within each guild.

On the lowest rung was the apprentice or trainee, usually aged about 12. After learning a trade for seven years, he would become a journeyman, working under a master craftsman. To become a master you had to prove to the guild that you had gained the necessary skill and experience, by producing a masterpiece.

The silk trade was unusual because more women were employed than in most guilds. This is an agreement for a girl entering the silk trade in 1392:

'This indenture witnesses that John Nougle of London, haberdasher, has put Katherine Nougle his sister apprentice to Avice Wodeford, silkthrower, of London to learn her art and to serve her after the manner of an apprentice from pentecost in the 15th year of the reign of King Richard II until the end of the next severn yeares...'

Workshop to Warfare, CUP, 1983, p.29

Some guilds provided care for members who grew old or ill and sometimes they set up and funded schools. Merchant Taylors' and Haberdashers schools, which still exist, owe their origins to guild schools.

Food and Drink

This description gives a picture of how feasts were conducted in the fifteenth century. Notice that forks are not mentioned: we may consider these to be basic but forks were not widely used until the seventeenth century. Instead people ate using spoons and knives. Plates were rarely used as food would be eaten off trenchers, 'plates' made of stale bread which soaked up the juices and could be fed either to the poor or the pigs afterwards!

'At feasts, first meat is prepared and arrayed, guests be called together, forms and stools be set in the hall, and tables, cloths and towels be ordained, disposed and made ready. Guests be set with the lord in the chief place of the board, and they sit not down at the board before the guests wash their hands. Children be set in their place, and servants at a table by themselves. First knives, spoons, and salts be set on the board, and then bread and drink, and many divers messes [dishes]... Now wine and messes of meat are brought forth and departed. At the last cometh fruit and spices, and when they have eaten, cloths and relief [trestles] are borne away...'

Bartholomew the Englishman, quoted in *A Baronial Household of the Thirteenth Century* by Margaret Wade Labarge, Harvester, 1980, p.121

Potatoes were unknown in Europe until the sixteenth century and so bread, made from a variety of grains, was the important staple food. The majority of people ate brown coarse bread made from barley, wheat, bran and rye.

A medieval banquet

Food at banquets could look spectacular – a peacock was roasted and then had most of its feathers replaced so that it looked alive.

Spices, dried fruits and nuts were frequently used by the cook to hide the taste of the salted – or, in some cases, rotting – meat and fish.

NTPL / ROB MATHESON

Manor houses (such as Ightham Mote in Kent, *left*), castles (such as Bodiam Castle in Sussex) and religious houses (such as Fountains Abbey in Yorkshire) had a supply of fresh fish from the moat or from fish ponds which were known as stews. Fresh fish tasted a lot better than the salted alternative!

Pigeon pie

During the winter months when there was a shortage of fresh meat, pigeon or 'squab' pie was a popular alternative, but only lords of the Manor had the right to own a dovecote for the birds to breed in.

The circular dovecotes at Cotehele in Cornwall and Avebury, Wiltshire are still standing. Monastic barns, like the Great Barn at Buckland Abbey, had nest boxes for pigeons.

Fish, fish or fish

The Church ruled that people should eat fish rather than meat on Wednesdays, Fridays, Saturdays and other holy days. This is what one schoolboy wrote complaining about his non-meat diet:

'You will not believe how tired I am of fish, and how much I wish that it was time to eat meat again, for during Lent I have eaten nothing but salted fish, it has gummed up my pipes so much that I can hardly breathe or speak.'

Fifteenth Century Schoolbook, quoted in *A Baronial Household of the Thirteenth Century*, p.179

Eat up your greens?

Vegetables were only eaten by the poor. In 1508, this is what the printer Wynkyn de Worde had to say about salad and fruit, foods which we now think are healthy:

'Beware of green sallettes and raw fruytes for they will make your soverayne seke [your body sick].'

The Boke of Kervynge quoted in *The Art of Dining*, Sara Paston-Williams, The National Trust, 1993, p.33

Thirstquenchers

Ale was made from barley, wheat or oats and was drunk at all times of the day, even at breakfast. Hops, from which most beer is made today, weren't introduced until the end of the Middle Ages.

The nobles and rich merchants drank wines from English vineyards or those imported from France, Portugal and Spain.

Disease and Medicine

A terrifying disease hit England in 1348. It soon spread to Wales, Ireland and parts of Scotland. Coming from Asia several years earlier, the plague was carried by fleas which lived on black rats, and had spread from the East along the trade routes.

The Black Death

'We see death coming into our midst like black smoke, a plague which cuts off the young, a rootless phantom which has no mercy for fair countenance. Woe is me of the shilling in the arm-pit; it is seething, terrible, wherever it may come, a head that gives pain and causes a loud cry, a burden carried under the arms, a painful angry knob, a white lump. It is of the form of an apple, like the head of an onion, a small boil that spares no one.'

Jeuan Gethin, Welsh poet, quoted in *The Black Death* by Philip Ziegler, Pelican, 1970, p.197

The plague spread rapidly amongst the poor who lived in cramped and unhygienic conditions. Monasteries were also badly hit. Some people thought that the Black Death was brought by the south wind so built their houses with windows only on the north side. The Black Death killed over half of the population.

'This plague slew Jew, Christian and Saracen alike; it carried off confessor and penitent together. In many places not even a fifth part of the people were left alive. It filled the whole world with terror. So great an epidemic has never been seen nor heard of before this time...'

The Black Death, p.185

Doctors, who were mostly untrained and not much help to the sick at the best of times, were reduced to trying anything:

'Toads should be thoroughly dried in the air or sun. They should be laid on the boil. Then the toad will swell and draw the poison of the plague through the skin to its own body.'

The Middle Ages by Jon Nichol & David Downton, Blackwell, 1981, p.23

Plague and punishment

Because people felt death could be just round the corner, many lived each day as if it were their last. Some decided that the only way to please God, whom they believed had sent the plague, was to show sorrow for their sins.

Those who survived the Black Death saw wages for labourers double, because of the shortage of workers. The salary rise for priests was even greater:

'Before the plague, for £3 a year a priest would live in a village and hold all the religious services. Now you have to pay up to £20 a year to get anybody to do the job.'

The Black Death, p.272

Medieval medicine

In the Middle Ages, people knew very little about the causes of sickness; they saw illness as God's punishment for sin and put their faith in the healing power of priests and prayers.

Medieval doctors believed that disease was caused by the different positions of the planets and 'bad blood'. Sick people were cut to let the blood escape or leeches were applied to suck it from them. In contrast, physicians in the Arab world were highly skilled and had a good knowledge of the working of the body. By the twelfth century one Arab physician had worked out how blood was pumped between the different chambers of the heart.

Herbal cures

Many minor illnesses were treated with a degree of success using herbal remedies, often put together by village wise women or by monks and nuns from their herb gardens. Blackberry leaves were good for sore throats while vinegar and honey, combined with garden clay, helped to cure boils.

A herb garden at Buckland Abbey in Devon still contains over 40 different herbs, such as rosemary, thyme, lad's love and feverfew.

Cloth and Dress

We can tell the styles of dress worn by people in the Middle Ages by looking at illuminated manuscripts, contemporary documents and letters, and at medieval tombs in churches.

Fine fabric or rough wool

The three or four metres of black velvet needed to make a gown might cost the same amount as a peasant earned in a whole year. Clothes were then considered very valuable possessions and would be handed down the generations.

While the rich wore clothes made of extravagant fabrics decorated with jewels, peasants produced their own wool which they would then weave into a coarse fabric and make up into rough, undyed clothes.

All the colours of the rainbow

The few surviving materials from medieval times have lost a great deal of their brilliance but we can tell from colourful manuscripts and descriptions that people loved bright clothes. There was a separate guild of tradesmen for dyeing cloth.

The Guildhall at Lavenham, a great medieval cloth-producing town in Suffolk, still has a garden containing some of the dye plants.

These are examples of where colours for dyeing cloth came from:

PLANTS
madder – red
woad – blue
dyers greenweed – yellow
indigo – blue

LICHEN
orchil – reddish purple

INSECTS
kermes – bright red
(expensive dye extracted from insects around the Mediterranean)
cochineal – deep red

Name that cloth

Luxury cloths were imported and their names give clues to where they came from. Damask, a heavy silk woven in a pattern, came from Damascus in Syria, while Baudekin, a heavy silk brocade, was brought from Baghdad, now in Iraq.

Local English woollen cloth was often known by the name of the town where it was produced, such as Coggeshall (Essex), or Taunton and Bridgewater (Somerset).

Knowing your place

Clothes were a way of showing where you stood in society. In 1336 guidelines were set down stating that only the royal family, earls, *prelates* (high-ranking churchmen), barons, knights and ladies with an income of at least £100 could wear fur.

People bought cloth and trimmings from a merchant, then took them to a tailor to be made up. Gowns were often trimmed or lined with fur – a necessity as castles and manor houses were cold and draughty. This is an extract from a letter written by Agnes Paston to her husband in the 1440s:

'The parson told me that if you would buy her a gown, her mother would give a good fur to trim it. The gown needs to be bought, and the colour ought to be a good blue or else a bright blood-red.'

The Pastons, Ed. Richard Barber, Penguin, 1981, p.18

Wash day

Cleaning and drying fabrics and clothes was a major operation and not done too often. A material for winter robes known as 'camlet', woven from camel's or goat's hair, had a very long *nap* (furry surface), so the best method was to shear a layer off when the top became dirty. This was a skilled job – the Countess of Leicester sent her gown of *perse* (a fine woollen cloth) to be shorn at a cost of 12 pence, plus two shillings for the tailor's expenses.

Other clothes were either soaked in water and beaten hard to shift the dirt, or soaked in a mixture known as lye. This was made from ash and water, or sometimes bird droppings, urine or bran!

Clothes were dried by twisting them tightly. In the eleventh century it was fashionable for women to wear clothes with tight pleats, reflecting this drying process.

Trade and the Crusades

While many people lived off the land and only needed to go to town to buy things they couldn't produce, such as salt and candles, there was a market for luxury and exotic goods amongst the wealthy. A trading network grew across Europe and the Middle East and once or twice a year merchants from all over the world gathered in large towns to sell their wares. Rich households would send their stewards hundreds of miles to buy up luxury goods and foods.

Exports

During the Middle Ages, wool was England's most valuable trading product. At first the raw wool was exported to the Continent to be woven. By 1310 England was exporting 40,000 sacks of wool a year. Raw wool had to pass through Calais on the way so that customs duties and taxes could be collected. This was called the Calais Staple.

Weaving gradually developed in England and by 1450 cloth was the kingdom's most important export.

While many old wool trade centres declined during the fifteenth century, Lavenham in Suffolk became one of the richest places in the country. Its Guildhall was built with profits from the wool trade and some wool and cloth merchants gave money to build entire churches.

The Crusades to the Middle East

In 1095 Pope Urban called on Christians across Europe to go on a crusade, to reclaim the religious sites of the Holy Land from the followers of Islam. The Church called their opponents 'the infidel', meaning 'no faith', but in fact the Muslims believed just as strongly in their right to protect their own holy places.

European knights responded to the Pope's call to arms. Some went for religious reasons, others hoped to gain wealth and land from taking part.

Even kings were prepared to fight in the crusades. England's Richard I, known as the Lionheart for his courage, was absent for many years. He left the country in the hands of his mother, Eleanor of Aquitaine, and almost lost his kingdom to his younger brother, John, as a result.

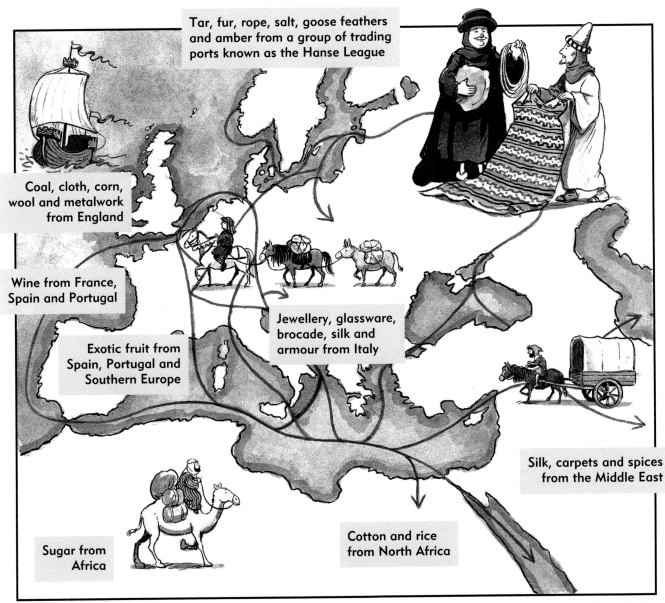

Tar, fur, rope, salt, goose feathers and amber from a group of trading ports known as the Hanse League

Coal, cloth, corn, wool and metalwork from England

Wine from France, Spain and Portugal

Exotic fruit from Spain, Portugal and Southern Europe

Jewellery, glassware, brocade, silk and armour from Italy

Silk, carpets and spices from the Middle East

Sugar from Africa

Cotton and rice from North Africa

The main trade routes around medieval Europe in about 1350

From crusade to trade

The crusaders finally failed to reclaim the Holy Land but the wars had a long-lasting effect on people's lives across Europe. The returning knights brought back new tastes for food and spices, knowledge of Arab medicine and inventions such as the windmill and the wheelbarrow.

There was a great deal of trade in cloths and spices with the Middle East but for most people it remained an area of mystery. This is how one thirteenth-century French knight thought spices were gathered:

'Before the river [Nile] enters into Egypt, people who are accustomed so to do, cast their nets out-spread into the river, at night, and when morning comes, they find in their nets such goods as are sold by weight, and brought into the land: ginger, rhubarb, herb of aloes, and cinnamon. And it is said that these things come from the earthly paradise.'

Baronial Household of the Thirteenth Century by Margaret Wade Labarge, Harvester, 1980, p.88

Life in a Medieval Town

In medieval England most people lived in the countryside. Between 1100 and 1300, roughly 170 new towns were established in England and Wales. Many grew up as castles and monasteries needed services around them; others grew as market towns, providing new wealth for the local lord.

Urban life

Many towns were walled for protection, so space was limited and building plots were expensive. As a result houses were often built several storeys high, with the upper storeys jutting out over the street. Only the richest could afford houses built of stone, so most were made of timber.

Towns were noisy and smelly places – people simply emptied their rubbish on to the street. In 1365 foreign traders refused to visit Lincoln until it had been cleaned! Streets could also be dangerous after dark and many town councils enforced a curfew – this meant that people had to stay indoors after dark.

The new boroughs

From the twelfth century leading traders organised Merchant Guilds and applied for a charter from the local lord, or even the king, which would grant them self-government of their town and the right to elect a council and mayor. The centre of administration was at the Guildhall and these powerful merchants were responsible for law and order in the borough.

There were strict rules about trading and many towns had a market court where punishments fitted the crime: for example, a trader who sold bad wine would have to drink it and then have the rest poured over his head.

Mystery plays

In the streets of some towns, guild members put on 'mystery' and miracle plays at certain times of the year (mystery was another name for trade or craft). These plays enacted stories from the Bible.

Town planning

The geographical location of a town was a key element in its eventual success or failure: good sites included busy cross-roads and safe harbours.

In the case of Winchelsea in Sussex, founded in 1088, a promising situation by the sea turned to disaster when the new settlement was struck by frequent flooding and attacks by the French. In the late thirteenth century the town was moved to higher ground but within a hundred years the sea had retreated so much that the harbour was too far inland, and Winchelsea was stranded from its sea trade route.

Market towns

With the permission of the king to hold a regular market, a lord could persuade craftworkers and merchants to move in and pay him rent.

Most towns held markets at least twice a week. Country people would bring their grain, livestock, eggs, milk and firewood to sell to the townspeople. They could then spend their profit on goods provided by the town craftworkers, such as shoes, pottery and cloth. Shops as we know them did not exist: the equivalent was a craft workshop.

What's in a name?

Streets were often named after the trade or craft worked in them, such as Silver Street or Baker's Lane. Many towns and cities still use street names dating from medieval times.

As so few people could read, pictorial signs were hung up outside workshops.

A large medieval town housed 2,000 people. How many live in your nearest town today?

Architecture

The style of architecture which was used for the building of churches and castles in the early Middle Ages is known as Romanesque. This style featured thick stone walls, small windows, round arches and huge pillars which supported the wooden roof.

A Norman arch at Fountains Abbey, Yorkshire

Cathedrals and castles

Strong and severe architecture partly reflected the uncertainty of times in which buildings were places to shelter from attack. The builders also felt that in order for the buildings to be stable, the walls had to be thick and not weakened by large windows.

During the twelfth century, builders discovered that with the help of flying buttresses as supports, it was possible to construct taller and thinner stone walls with larger windows. They also realised that by using vaulting *(see right)* the roof was self-supporting, so thick round pillars were no longer necessary. Churches and cathedrals became more and more ornate, with lots of stone carving and decoration – this was known as the Gothic style.

Tattershall Castle in Lincolnshire, built around 1440

NTPL / BRIAN LAWRENCE

Stained glass

With the Gothic style came an opportunity for glaziers to show their skills at creating huge stained glass windows.

All glass was blown by hand and so there was a limit to the size of each piece. In order to fill the space created for a window, coloured glass pieces were carefully arranged, painted with details and joined with lead strips to form a large pattern.

Wattle and daub

Buildings of stone were reserved for the very wealthy. In southern England most people's houses were built of wooden frames with walls made out of *wattle and daub* (a mixture of mud, dung and straw plastered over a framework of twigs). These buildings were not as long-lasting as those built of stone so there are very few surviving houses from this period. In other parts of the country timber was not always available and mud and slate were used.

Alfriston Clergy House in Sussex is a rare example of a medieval timber-framed house, dating back to the middle of the fourteenth century.

NTPL / ROB MATHESON

Tithe barn at Great Coxwell, Berkshire

Tithe barns

These were used to house the *tithe* (the proportion of each peasant's harvest of grain owed to the Church). They were often huge buildings – the one at Buckland Abbey in Devon is nearly 49 metres long and its walls are nearly a metre thick.

Moated manor houses

Many manor houses of the medieval period were fortified as it was a time of great unrest. An effective defence was a moat. Houses like Baddesley Clinton and Ightham Mote in Kent still have moats today.

Manor houses were often built to a courtyard plan, with large windows looking on to the courtyard. However, the walls looking out to the surrounding country would have had smaller windows which were easier to defend from attackers.

Baddesley Clinton in Warwickshire

Places to Visit

Here are some National Trust places which were built in medieval times, although many have been altered since then:

Alfriston Clergy House, East Sussex
A timber-framed thatched building, constructed in about 1350.

Baddesley Clinton, Warwickshire
A moated manor house built in the fifteenth century.

Bodiam Castle, East Sussex
Built as a grand home in the 1380s because of the threat of invasion. The moat is still full of water and there are lots of winding staircases.

Buckland Abbey, Devon
Built as a Cistercian Abbey in 1278. The medieval church and great barn can still be seen.

Chirk Castle, Wrexham
A magnificent fortress completed in 1310 and occupied ever since.

Corfe Castle, Dorset
The ruins of a castle built mainly in the twelfth and thirteenth centuries.

Fountains Abbey, Yorkshire
The ruin of a twelfth-century Cistercian Abbey sheltered in a secluded valley. Part of a World Heritage Site.

Ightham Mote, Kent
A moated courtyard house set in a wooded valley, dating originally from the fourteenth century.

Lacock Abbey, Wiltshire
Founded as a nunnery in 1232 but converted into a private house after the Dissolution of the Monasteries.

Little Moreton Hall, Cheshire
A perfect example of a timber-framed moated house. The oldest parts, including the Great Hall, were built around 1450.

Oxburgh Hall, Norfolk
A moated courtyard house built in the late fifteenth century, with a splendid turreted gatehouse.

Tattershall Castle, Lincolnshire
A vast fortified tower built for Henry VI's Treasurer.

Cotehele in Cornwall is built around a series of courtyards and reached through a medieval gatehouse.

For a full list of National Trust properties, see *The National Trust Handbook*, available from National Trust shops and good book shops.

COVER PICTURES
(clockwise from top left): An illuminated manuscript (NTPL / ANGELO HORNAK); Monks at Fountains Abbey; Peasant boy at work on the harvest; Knights jousting; A medieval ring brooch; Bodiam Castle in Sussex (NTPL / OLIVER BENN); A noblewoman reads aloud.

First published in 1997 by National Trust (Enterprises) Ltd, 36 Queen Anne's Gate, London SW1H 9AS

Registered Charity No. 205846

ISBN 0 7078 0226 1

Designed by Gill Mouqué

Printed on environmentally friendly paper by Waterside Press, England

The National Curriculum

Investigating Medieval Times provides useful background information for children covering a medieval local history topic (**Key Stage 2**: Study Unit 5a or b), or *Medieval realms: Britain 1066-1500* (**Key Stage 3**: Study Unit 1).